Text TM & copyright © by Dr. Seuss Enterprises, L.P. 1980
Cover art and interior illustrations copyright © 2020 by Kelly Kennedy

All rights reserved. Published in the United States by Random House Children's Books,
a division of Penguin Random House LLC, New York. Originally published in the
United States in a different form by Random House Children's Books, a division of
Penguin Random House LLC, New York, in 1980.

Beginner Books, Random House, and the Random House colophon are registered
trademarks of Penguin Random House LLC. The Cat in the Hat logo ® and
© Dr. Seuss Enterprises, L.P. 1957, renewed 1986. All rights reserved.

Visit us on the Web!
Seussville.com
rhcbooks.com

Educators and librarians, for a variety of teaching tools, visit us at
RHTeachersLibrarians.com

Library of Congress Cataloging-in-Publication Data is available upon request.

ISBN 978-1-9848-9406-9 (trade) — ISBN 978-1-9848-9407-6 (lib. bdg.)

MANUFACTURED IN CHINA
10 9 8 7 6
First Edition

# Dr. Seuss

## Maybe You Should FLY a JET!

## Maybe You Should BE a VET!

illustrated by Kelly Kennedy

BEGINNER BOOKS®
A Division of Random House

# Want to be a ticket taker?

# Want to be a pizza maker?

General

Jockey

Basketball player

Ballet dancer

Dragon slayer

Do you want to be an astronaut?
Or keeper of the zoo?

You've got to do something.
What DO you want to do?

# Tailor?

# Sailor?

# Nailer?

# Jailer?

You've got to BE someone
sooner or later.
How about
a wrestler . . .

a welder . . .

or a waiter?

How about
a dentist?

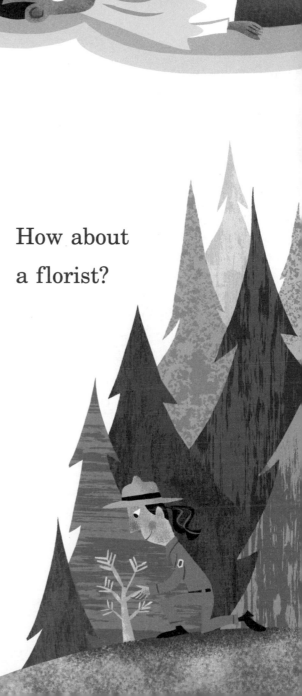

How about
a florist?

How about
a forester
working in a forest?

Do you wish to be an oil refiner?

Diamond miner?

Dress designer?

How about a paper hanger?

How about a bass drum banger?

# Do you want to do your work outdoors?

## Do you want to work inside?

# Would you like to be a plumber?

## A stargazer? A mountain guide?

Would you rather work
in a mountain town . . .

or in the desert
lower down?

You could be a turkey farmer.

You could be a teacher.

You could be a lot of things.
How about a preacher?

You could be a clown!

Or a coffee perker!

How about

an ironworker?

Some folks make
good picture framers.

Some folks make
good lion tamers.

Some folks make good tightrope walkers.

Other folks
are better talkers.

# Maybe you should fly a jet.

# Maybe you should be a vet.

How about a
deep-sea diver?

How about a
beehive hiver?

Would you like to be an actor?

Would you like to run a tractor?

# Like to drive a taxicab?

# Or run a big computer lab?

Tennis pro . . .

Optometrist

Crossing guard . . .

Podiatrist

# Chemist . . .

# Lepidopterist

# Glassblower

# Mushroom grower

How about a
fishbone boner

or a roller coaster
owner?

Would you sooner
be a ballooner

or a grand-piano tuner?

Olympic champ?

Reporter of the news?
It's very difficult
to choose.

You've got to be someone!
You can't just be a doodler.
You could be
a sculptor . . .

or, perhaps,
a noodle noodler.

You might be
a private eye!

Would you like
to be a spy?

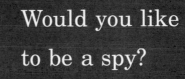

Maybe you should be
a vester . . .

a jester

or a hammock tester.

Maybe you should be
a voice.
Someday you must
make a choice.
Maybe you should be
a FOICE!

When you find out
what a FOICE is,
you can tell us
what your choice is.